THE
WHIZ
QUIZ
BOOK

For Children and Grown-up Children

THE WHIZ QUIZ BOOK

For Children and Grown-up Children

Compiled by the Cork West Branch
of the NPC-P

The Collins Press

PUBLISHED IN 2016 BY
The Collins Press
West Link Park
Doughcloyne
Wilton
Cork
T12 N5EF
Ireland

FIRST EDITION 2000
SECOND EDITION 2005

A Cataloguing-in-Publication data record for this book is available
from the British Library

ISBN: 978-184889-297-2

Typesetting by The Collins Press
Font: AGaramond, 11 point

Printed in Poland by Drukarnia Skleniarz

ACKNOWLEDGEMENTS

The following people have contributed to the compilation of this quiz book, which took us over twelve months to put together. For all their time, help and continued interest, we are very grateful and offer them our thanks.

Thanks to all the principals, teachers and children, from the following schools, who contributed questions: Aghina, Ballinora, Clogheen/Kerry Pike, Cloghroe and Rylane. Thanks to Dan O'Donovan who provided quiz questions each year for the NPC Challenge Quiz from which our idea of an Irish quiz book was conceived; to Ann Rea for arranging all the questions into rounds and who, together with Ann O'Regan and Lorraine Crossan, typed up the various drafts; to Marty Mainerich who revised some of the original questions for this new edition; and lastly, to all the members of NPC-P Cork West who proofread all the draft submissions.

INTRODUCTION

The Whiz Quiz Book is a product of *partnership in education* at its best. Not only were parents and teachers involved in researching this work but the most important partners of all, i.e., the children, had a significant input, in terms of content and design.

The book is a response to a widespread demand among parents and teachers for 'lists of questions', particularly in the lead up to National Parents Council's popular annual quiz, the NPC-Challenge.

The questions are tailored to the abilities of children in primary, or in the early years of second level schools. They are formatted into a series of *mini competitions* which can provide competitive, educative entertainment in the family home, the classroom or wherever groups of friends may meet.

Cork West have several years of experience as quiz organisers and that experience is reflected in this very excellent publication.

CON LYNCH
NATIONAL VICE-CHAIRMAN, NPC-P

QUIZ NUMBER 1

ROUND 1

1. Where was Christopher Columbus born: Lisbon, Genoa or Madrid?

2. What time shows a quarter to seven pm on the 24-hour clock?

3. What sort of ship would fly a Jolly Roger?

4. What was Cuchulainn's name before he was called Cuchulainn?

5. In the *Jungle Book* what kind of animal is Baloo?

6. Name the highest point in Donegal?

7. Silken Thomas was a famous character in Irish history. What was his surname?

8. *Cén sórt rud é 'Ceirnín*?

Answers on page 101

ROUND 2

1. Which islands in the Atlantic Ocean have the same name as a bird?

2. What was Batman's secret identity?

3. What three letters are usually used to describe deoxyribonucleic acid?

4. In Greek legend, who killed the Minotaur?

5. In what year was University College Cork founded?

6. What Irish battle took place in the year 1601?

7. If you were born on 1 April, what would your star sign be?

8. Give the proper term for the direction a bishop moves in the game of chess?

Answers on page 101

ROUND 3

1. In what year was Saoirse Ronan nominated for an Oscar for her performance in the film *Brooklyn*?

2. In Irish folklore who was Oisín's father?

3. What was the title of the 2015 *Star Wars* film partly filmed on the Skellig Islands?

4. Name the largest county in the province of Ulster?

5. What does nocturnal mean?

6. During which war did Anne Frank write her diary while living in the attic of a house in Amsterdam?

7. Finish the well-known phrase 'A stitch in time ...'

8. What were Ancient Egyptian tombs called?

Answers on page 101

Round 4

1. What profession does the INTO represent?

2. In what city in Ireland is Eyre Square?

3. What are animals who mainly feed on grasses, shrubs and heathers called?

4. Who wrote the play *The Countess Cathleen*?

5. What is the capital city of Norway?

6. In the nursery rhyme 'Hey Diddle Diddle', what did the dish do?

7. In which part of the body would you find the anvil, the hammer and the stirrup?

8. What letter represents 1,000 in Roman numerals?

Answers on page 101

ROUND 5

1. In mathematics, what does LCM stand for?

2. What type of creature was Pegasus?

3. In which county is the Giant's Causeway?

4. What hormone controls the supply of sugar from the blood to the muscles?

5. The house situated at no. 1,600 Pennsylvania Avenue is better known as what?

6. How many months have 31 days?

7. In *Teenage Mutant Ninja Turtles*, what is April's surname?

8. What is the only bird that can fly backwards?

Answers on page 101

ROUND 6

1. Who was the first man in space in 1961?

2. In which novel does the ghost of Jacob Morley make an appearance?

3. How many O.W.L.s did Harry Potter receive?

4. In the term e-mail, what does the e stand for?

5. Who uses the code name 007?

6. Leonardo da Vinci's portrait of 'Lisa del Giocondra' is better known as what?

7. In what county are the Maamturk Mountains?

8. Where was Eamon de Valera born?

Answers on page 101

Round 7

1. Who wrote the poem that includes the line 'I wandered lonely as a cloud'?

2. How much money do you get for passing 'Go' in the game of Monopoly?

3. If you were born on 1 January what would your star sign be?

4. What is the name of the girl who went with Oisín to Tir-Na-nÓg?

5. Who invented the miner's safety lamp?

6. What was the title of Nathan Carter's first album?

7. For which sport is the Ryder Cup awarded?

8. Who is the school principal in the children's novel *Matilda*?

Answers on page 102

Round 8

1. Who scored Ireland's winning goal against Italy in the 2016 UEFA European Championship?

2. In what language was 'Silent Night' originally written?

3. Which sea in the Middle East is so salty that nothing can live in it?

4. What do the scales of Fahrenheit and Celsius measure?

5. Who first brought potatoes to Ireland?

6. In *Cinderella*, what vegetable did the Fairy Godmother turn into a coach?

7. Who is the patron saint of Wales?

8. In Irish mythology, who caught the salmon of knowledge?

Answers on page 102

ROUND 9

1. In which continent are the Atlas Mountains?

2. In which county is Vinegar Hill?

3. Herons usually nest in large colonies known as what?

4. What is the telephone dialling code for Limerick?

5. What is the name given to substances which are responsible for most of the colours in plants and animals?

6. With which kind of meat would you normally serve mint sauce?

7. What is the name of the village in *Fireman Sam*?

8. On which Irish hill did St Patrick light the Pascal Fire?

Answers on page 102

Round 10

1. What significant event in Irish history happened in 1607?

2. Name the author of the Famous Five series of books?

3. How many sides has a snowflake?

4. At what age are you legally entitled to vote in the Irish Republic?

5. Which river flows into the sea at Kinsale in County Cork?

6. On which river was the salmon of knowledge caught?

7. Name the famous couple who honeymooned in 2014 at Castle Oliver in County Limerick, Ballyfin House in County Laois and Castlemartyr Resort in County Cork.

8. Who was the manager of the Republic of Ireland soccer team that beat Italy in the 2016 UEFA European Championship?

Answers on page 102

Quiz Number 2
Round 1

1. In Irish folklore, what bird is thought to be king?

2. What finger boasts the fastest growing nail?

3. What famous English naturalist wrote a book called *The Origin of the Species* in 1859?

4. What is the highest number in the national lottery?

5. Summer Bay is the setting for which television series?

6. What name is given to the imaginary line 23.5⁰ south of the equator?

7. In ancient Irish history where did the Celts come from?

8. Off what county is Tory Island?

Answers on page 103

ROUND 2

1. What is the name of the main character in the Tomb Raider computer games?

2. What oil is obtained from flax?

3. In which county is Fota Wildlife Park situated?

4. What is the sport of exploring caves called?

5. What country issued the first postage stamp?

6. The historical epic 'Braveheart', which was directed by Mel Gibson on location in Ireland, is about the life of which Scottish figure?

7. Is a cat a biped, triped or quadruped?

8. What is the capital of Kenya?

Answers on page 103

ROUND 3

1. Does a peach have a stone, a bean or pips?

2. In what county is the Glen of Imaal?

3. What organs extract oxygen from the air?

4. What is a young male horse called?

5. How many pints are in a gallon?

6. What is dried to make a sultana?

7. In what year was the All-Ireland Football Final played in New York?

8. Where did Samson's strength lie?

Answers on page 103

ROUND 4

1. Which number is at the top of a dartboard?

2. What is the capital of Madagascar?

3. Where is the International Court of Justice?

4. Festivals are held in Galway and Clarinbridge every year around September celebrating which of the following (a) jazz (b) film (c) oysters?

5. Which animal is said to have a cross on its back to mark its journey with Jesus into Jerusalem?

6. With which musical instrument do we associate Caroline Corr?

7. Who wrote the series of books about Narnia?

8. In which country is the tomb of Tutankhamun?

Answers on page 103

Round 5

1. In which city did the Last Supper take place?

2. In what county is the town of Nenagh?

3. For which team did Roy Keane play before he was transferred to Manchester United?

4. *Merci Beaucoup a deirtear sa bhFraincis – cad é seo as Gaeilge?*

5. Who was the President of the United States of America (USA) during the American Civil War?

6. What do the letters NPC-P stand for?

7. In *Babar and the Adventures of Badou*, what is the name of Babar's wife?

8. What does the Roman numeral C stand for?

Answers on page 103

ROUND 6

1. In maths what does the word 'mean' mean?

2. What is the largest island in the world?

3. What was the name of the cub in the Disney film who eventually became the 'Lion King'?

4. What is a male goat called?

5. In what county are the Marble Arch Caves – Fermanagh, Derry or Sligo?

6. Who writes the comic strip 'Garfield'?

7. What was the name of Hitler's secret police?

8. On what day of the week did Christ ascend into heaven?

Answers on page 103

Round 7

1. How many sides has a pentagon?

2. What is the capital of Tazmania?

3. What kind of food does the badger eat?

4. How many teeth should an adult have?

5. What ball game played indoors and outdoors was invented in Canada in 1896?

6. In music a minim has two beats. What do you call a note with one beat?

7. In what county is the Corraun Peninsula?

8. What name is commonly given to jets of hot water forced out of the ground?

Answers on page 103

Round 8

1. What historical figure do we associate with Avondale, County Wicklow?

2. What two colours would an artist mix to make green?

3. What animal did Noah allegedly leave behind from the Ark?

4. Who wrote the book *The Hobbit*?

5. Where would you find an epitaph written?

6. What Irishman ordered that his epitaph not be written until his country was free?

7. Is rounders an Olympic sport?

8. Name the Chinese medical treatment that involves needles?

Answers on page 104

ROUND 9

1. What is the national flower of Austria?

2. Which are usually the smallest chess pieces?

3. Waterford city stands beside what river?

4. Who was the famous illustrator of Roald Dahl's books?

5. Who was Britain's first female Prime Minister?

6. From what metal was the mask of Tutankhamun made?

7. What county's vehicle registration code is represented by WH?

8. Which planet in our solar system is closest to the earth?

Answers on page 104

ROUND 10

1. Name the famous outlaw who lived in Sherwood Forest?

2. Name the author of the book *Boy*?

3. Who invented television?

4. What is the real name of U2's guitarist 'The Edge'?

5. In which province is the borough of Fingal?

6. Which Roman official ordered the execution of Christ?

7. Who was the only Irish president to resign?

8. What is the name of the tunnel under the River Lee?

Answers on page 104

QUIZ NUMBER 3

ROUND 1

1. Is a baby whale called a fishlet, a calf or a kipper?

2. Which fruit do many athletes eat to give instant energy before a race?

3. In what country was the War of the Roses?

4. In what month are the All-Ireland Hurling and Football Finals usually held?

5. Who directed the films 'ET' and 'Jurassic Park'?

6. What name is given to a craft which floats on top of a cushion of air?

7. What country is known as the land of the rising sun?

8. Name the four teenagers who solve mysteries in the Scooby-Doo series.

Answers on page 104

Round 2

1. Who made the famous voyage with three ships, *The Nina, The Pinta* and the *Santa Maria*?

2. In mathematics, what does the abbreviation HCF stand for?

3. Finish the phrase 'The hand that rocks the cradle ...'

4. Which is used as a rest in snooker – a fly, a beetle or a spider?

5. Which black and white birds can swim faster than any others?

6. What country do people reach if they swim the Channel from France?

7. What fabled Irish king hated hair cuts?

8. Why?

Answers on page 104

ROUND 3

1. During which two seasons are the equinoxes – spring and autumn, or summer and winter?

2. *Cad is brí leis an bhfocal 'turas?*

3. Which famous detective lived on Baker Street in London?

4. If a + 46 = 109 - b; and b = 27, what is a?

5. Name the Irish race walker who was uprgraded to a bronze Olympic medal in 2016.

6. What is the name of the alphabet for the blind which uses various combinations of up to six raised dots to represent different letters and figures?

7. In what Australian city does the government sit?

8. In which county is Glendalough situated?

Answers on page 104

Round 4

1. Name the pub in Coronation Street?

2. The Pacific and Atlantic are two of the world's great oceans. Name two others.

3. Is a tomato a fruit or a vegetable?

4. Who was nominated by Eamon de Valera to be the first president of Ireland?

5. In which American State is the Grand Canyon – Arizona, Colorado, Nevada or New Mexico?

6. How did Icarus escape from Crete?

7. In the parliament of the United Kingdom, what is the Upper House called?

8. What is celebrated in France on 14 July every year?

Answers on page 105

ROUND 5

1. What is the young of a frog called?

2. In the Bible, what queen visited King Solomon?

3. What instrument does James Galway play?

4. What is the capital city of the Czech Republic?

5. Where specifically in the body is your thyroid?

6. Newcastlewest is in which Irish county?

7. Who was shot and killed in Dallas, Texas in 1963?

8. What branch of crop growing deals with garden and green houses?

Answers on page 105

Round 6

1. Who was the first Irishman to win an Oscar for Best Original Song?

2. In which direction are you facing if a southerly wind is blowing on your back?

3. Which animal gives its name to the rugby team made up of players from Britain, Ireland, Scotland and Wales?

4. In which book does the character Long John Silver appear?

5. Which elephant has the larger ears, African or Indian?

6. In what county is Athenry?

7. Drake Passage is off the southern end of what continent?

8. Who wrote the novel *PS I Love You*?

Answers on page 105

Round 7

1. Name the fictional hero of the set of books written by J.K. Rowling?

2. Was Mary McAleese the seventh, eighth or ninth president of Ireland?

3. Name the legendary brothers who were reared by a wolf and who founded Rome?

4. Which ship was the first to send out an SOS?

5. If you suffer from anosmia, what would be your problem?

6. What is 90 squared?

7. Banna Strand is in what county?

8. In what year was the first space shuttle launched?

Answers on page 105

Round 8

1. What name is given to the piece of wood which supports the strings on a violin?

2. In the Bible, whose Gospel first appears in the New Testament?

3. What is the southernmost point on the island of Ireland?

4. Who was the first Taoiseach of Ireland?

5. What liquid, which is used in thermometers, is also known as quick silver?

6. In which year did RTE television begin broadcasting – 1961, 1962 or 1963?

7. The country of Mozambique is in which continent?

8. Is judo ability measured in dans, dons or dins?

Answers on page 105

ROUND 9

1. How long is the term of office of a president in the USA?

2. Where is the sea of tranquillity?

3. In what county are the Japanese Gardens?

4. Who created Frankenstein?

5. Where was the first Marathon run?

6. What was the name of King Arthur's wife?

7. What famous golf course is in Liscannor Bay, County Clare?

8. Who plays Lara Croft in the 'Tomb Raider' films?

Answers on page 105

Round 10

1. What was the name of the ship on which there was a famous mutiny against Captain Bligh?

2. What position is the head of the UN?

3. Sofia is the capital of which eastern European country?

4. What is the Least Common Multiple of the numbers 3 and 4?

5. What is the common name for a pleasant smelling mixture of alcohol and oils?

6. Name the longest river in Britain?

7. Who said, 'That's one small step for man, one giant step for mankind'?

8. Mount Everest is the highest peak on earth. Of where is Olympus Mans the highest peak?

Answers on page 105

QUIZ NUMBER 4

ROUND 1

1. In the film 'Into the West', what was the name of the horse?

2. Who wrote *Alice's Adventures in Wonderland*?

3. What fruit is named after a New Zealand bird?

4. What is the smallest county in Munster?

5. What is a young eel called?

6. What is the vitamin which we get from sunlight?

7. Which sport is controlled by an organisation called FIFA?

8. In Irish folklore, who had a dog named Bran?

Answers on page 106

Round 2

1. What are the seven colours of the rainbow?

2. Is a dolphin a fish or a mammal?

3. *Cad is brí leis an bhfocal 'Ríomhaire*?

4. What is the largest lake in Ireland?

5. The Statue of Liberty was a gift to America from what European country?

6. Where are the Slieve Mish Mountains?

7. What is measured in decibels?

8. In the Harry Potter series, what subject does Professor Trelawney teach?

Answers on page 106

ROUND 3

1. What name is given to the period of the earth's geological history when it was covered in large sheets of ice?

2. Name the gas that helps to keep the earth warm?

3. What city is famous for its leaning tower?

4. In the world of cartoons, in what town do Fred Flintstone and Barney Rubble live?

5. What animal is celebrated in Killorglin, County Kerry, every year?

6. Lent is the name given to the period leading up to Easter. What is the period leading up to Christmas called?

7. Who writes the series of books called *The Babysitters Club*?

8. In which county is the town of Lurgan?

Answers on page 106

ROUND 4

1. What is the capital of Greece?

2. Complete the proverb 'A chain is as strong as ...'

3. Cos and iceberg are types of what vegetable?

4. Which game is being played if advantage follows deuce?

5. What is the name of Mickey Mouse's dog?

6. What is a female seal called?

7. In *The Simpsons*, what is Milhouse's surname?

8. Name Northern Ireland's only inhabited island?

Answers on page 106

Round 5

1. If you walked down 'Ramsey Street' what TV Programme would you be in?

2. *Cad é an focal Gaeilge ar* 'clouds'?

3. What is amnesia?

4. Who wrote the series of books known as *The Hunger Games*?

5. In what year was the last battle of the Crusades fought?

6. Which is the largest of the Balearic Islands?

7. Who writes *Sweet Valley Twins*?

8. During which World War were tanks first used?

Answers on page 106

ROUND 6

1. Mary Stuart was queen of which country?

2. What Emperor hung the 'Mona Lisa' in his bathroom?

3. Who wrote the play *Dancing at Lughnasa*?

4. Is New Zealand, southeast or southwest of Australia?

5. In what year was the Battle of Clontarf fought?

6. Who was the Greek god of love?

7. In maths, if x - 7 = 8, what is x?

8. What is palaeontology?

Answers on page 106

ROUND 7

1. Who was the president of the USA prior to Barack Obama?

2. In Walt Disney's film '101 Dalmations', name either of Cruella's two henchmen.

3. In what county in Ireland is the town of Skibbereen?

4. Which planet lies nearest the sun?

5. Who wrote *The Odyssey*?

6. What are Stilton and Brie?

7. Kingstown is now known by what name?

8. What sport are you playing if you shout 'Fore' to warn people that you have hit the ball?

Answers on page 106

ROUND 8

1. What is the national symbol of Scotland?

2. What crime novelist occasionally wrote romantic novels under the pen-name Mary Westmacott?

3. When did C.J. Haughey first become Taoiseach – 1975, 1979 or 1981?

4. What name is given to the distance which (a beam of) light travels in a year?

5. What is the capital of Equador?

6. What number is on top of the dice if four is at the bottom?

7. What do you score in cricket if you score goals in football?

8. Who wrote the famous novel *Black Beauty*?

Answers on page 107

Round 9

1. What is the collective term for a group of whales?

2. Which way do stalactites grow – up or down?

3. What part of you is affected if you suffer from cardio-vascular disease?

4. The British Prime Minister lives at No. 10 Downing Street. Who lives at No. 11?

5. In which American state are the cities of Orlando, Jacksonville and Miami?

6. Name the last Irishman to win the Nobel Prize for Literature?

7. Where was the first wooden church in Ireland built?

8. In what country was Roald Dahl born?

Answers on page 107

ROUND 10

1. What saint had a vision of the Virgin Mary at Lourdes in 1858?

2. What was the name of the strange kind of pictorial writing used by ancient Egyptians?

3. What letter represents 50 in Roman numerals?

4. How does a sun-dial help tell the time?

5. Is most of a Jumbo Jet's fuel stored in the tail, the wings or the bulkhead?

6. What do we call the pattern left inside a rock by an ancient animal or plant?

7. Name the king who appears in the book about Narnia.

8. In which country is the Taj Mahal?

Answers on page 107

QUIZ NUMBER 5

ROUND 1

1. Springfield is the home of which TV family?

2. What is a female fox called?

3. Which Irish county is known as the Premier County?

4. In which city is the headquarters of the United Nations situated?

5. The song 'You've got to pick a pocket or two' comes from what musical?

6. In Irish mythology, Eimear was the wife of which hero?

7. Who was the first woman to fly across the Atlantic in an aeroplane?

8. How many of the nine people in each boat face forwards during a boat race?

Answers on page 107

ROUND 2

1. Which black powder is produced when you burn coal?

2. What do the sperm, humpback and pilot all have in common?

3. Distance north and south of the equator is measured by lines of (a) longitude or (b) latitude?

4. Who walked to London with his cat?

5. What is the capital city of Austria?

6. Who wrote the novels, *Pride and Prejudice*, *Emma* and *Persuasion*?

7. Who is missing from the list, Doc, Sneezy, Happy, Grumpy, Sleepy and Dopey?

8. Which ball is worth the most points in a game of snooker?

Answers on page 107

ROUND 3

1. How many legs has a spider?

2. Name the fruit of the blackthorn tree?

3. In which book by Charles Dickens is there a dog called Jip?

4. What is the study of time called?

5. What was the Gae Bolga?

6. How many counties are there in the province of Ulster?

7. Which canal links the Atlantic and Pacific Oceans?

8. What woman wiped the face of Jesus on the way to Calvary?

Answers on page 107

Round 4

1. A winklepicker is a type of what? Is it (a) a shoe; (b) a wild pig or (c) a variety of vegetable?

2. *Lundi* is the French word for what day of the week?

3. Former actor Arnold Schwarzenegger is a native of what country?

4. Which would win a 100 metres race – an athlete, an ostrich or a greyhound?

5. What country is the largest producer of gold, platinum and diamonds?

6. Name one ball and socket joint in the body.

7. What is the home of an otter called?

8. According to the legend, what happened to anybody that looked directly at Medusa?

Answers on page 108

Round 5

1. What is the largest island off the Irish Coast?

2. Is your patella in your (a) wrist; (b) leg or (c) ear? ‾

3. Name either of the two meats normally used in an Irish stew?

4. What type of boot is named after a famous British soldier and Prime Minister?

5. What famous patriot was secretly engaged to Sarah Curran?

6. Name two of the Famous Five characters?

7. Niamh Cassidy, Paul Brennan, Leo Dowling and Bela Doyle are all characters on what television series?

8. *Little Women*, by Louisa May Alcott, is set in what location?

Answers on page 108

Round 6

1. In olden times in Ireland, what was a druid?

2. How many pieces are on the board at the beginning of a game of draughts?

3. How long would you be married if you were celebrating your Silver Wedding Anniversary?

4. What letter and number are used to identify the main road route from Dublin to Wexford?

5. In Greek mythology, who was the father of all the gods?

6. Manila is the capital of which country?

7. In *Shaun the Sheep*, what is the name of the farmer's sheepdog?

8. If you were a somnambulist, what would you be apt to do?

Answers on page 108

Round 7

1. What word can you put in front of the following to change their meaning: cup; milk; scotch?

2. The water carrier represents what sign on the Zodiac?

3. Her real name is Destiny Hope Cyrus. By what name is she better known?

4. Name the Swedish chemist who invented powerful explosives and gives his name to a world famous prize?

5. What is the capital town of County Clare?

6. How many points are scored for getting a dart in the small ring around the bull's-eye?

7. In the Bible, is the Book of Esther part of the Old or New Testament?

8. In what county is Cong Abbey?

Answers on page 108

Round 8

1. What does the abbreviation CFC stand for?

2. What is the largest country in the world?

3. In which European city is the Atomium?

4. Aberdeen Angus are a breed of what?

5. Neil Armstrong was the first man to step onto the Moon. Who was the second?

6. Amy Huberman *is bean chéile do cé hé*?

7. In military terms what do the letters AWOL mean?

8. Name the instrument that singer/songwriter Elton John normally plays?

Answers on page 108

Round 9

1. What is the largest desert in the world? Is it (a) Antarctica (b) Sahara or (c) Gobi Desert?

2. What is the black bit in the middle of your eye called?

3. How many people are there on a volleyball team?

4. What is the highest mountain in Leinster?

5. What word describes a regular movement of animals to and from certain places?

6. Is tea made from a leaf, a bean or a root?

7. Which king was famous for his wisdom?

8. What is the largest state in the USA?

Answers on page 108

ROUND 10

1. How many sides has an octagon?

2. What is the main colour of the Earth when looked at from space?

3. Which Irish saint was known as the Navigator?

4. In the film, 'The Wizard of Oz', what was the straw man looking for?

5. What musical instrument was associated with the late Louis Armstrong?

6. What is mozzarella?

7. Where did the first miracle performed by Jesus take place?

8. Who wrote the series of books about Adrian Mole?

Answers on page 108

Quiz Number 6

Round 1

1. What band did Robbie Williams first play with before his solo career?

2. German brothers Karl and Theo Albrecht founded which supermarket?

3. *Bhí an cat ag seinm ar an veidhlín, bhí an madra ag gáire and d'imigh an mias leis an spúnóg. Cé léim thar an ngealach?*

4. Who wrote the *Twilight* series of books?

5. Which is further west – Rome or Stockholm?

6. What organisation did Douglas Hyde and Eoin MacNeill form in 1893?

7. In what year was the storming of the Bastille?

8. On what racecourse is the English Grand National run?

Answers on page 109

ROUND 2

1. Who did Barcelona defeat in the 2015 UEFA Champions League final?

2. Who sent the first telegraph message?

3. What are otter droppings called?

4. What name is given to a baby kangaroo?

5. What creature is a Rhode Island Red?

6. What is the capital of Bulgaria?

7. What piece of computer hardware connects a computer to the Internet?

8. The Roman emperor Caligula appointed his horse to the Senate. True or False?

Answers on page 109

Round 3

1. Who played the role of James Bond in the film *Skyfall*?

2. Where did King Arthur hold court?

3. Benito Mussolini led what country during the Second World War?

4. Is the changing shape of the moon called its (a) phrases; (b) phases or (c) lasers?

5. Where is Oscar Wilde buried?

6. What does the German word *wilkommen* mean?

7. What is the county town of Westmeath?

8. In which country is the Jutland Peninsula?

Answers on page 109

Round 4

1. Name the ship Sir Francis Drake sailed in on his voyage around the world?

2. Who was known as the Serpent of the Nile?

3. The Garda Síochana was established in the 1920s, 1930s or 1940s?

4. What is the third planet out from the sun in the solar system?

5. In what country was Pope John Paul II born?

6. Red Admiral, Peacock and Cabbage White are all types of what?

7. *Cad is brí leis an bhfocal 'Cathair'?*

8. What were first issued in 1950 and allowed people to purchase goods and services by plastic?

Answers on page 109

Round 5

1. In the *Pirates of the Caribbean* films, Orlando Bloom plays which character?

2. What is the correct term for the arms of an octopus?

3. With which sport do you associate Darren Clarke and Tiger Woods?

4. What did Anne Frank call her diary?

5. Who was the first film star featured on a postage stamp?

6. Name the smallest of the Aran Islands.

7. In what year was the Battle of the Boyne?

8. What name is given to a space that is totally empty?

Answers on page 109

ROUND 6

1. Who writes the *Goosebumps* series of young people's books?

2. Which of the seven wonders of the ancient world is still standing?

3. On what river is Belfast built?

4. Jim Henson, the puppeteer, who died in 1990 was responsible for what TV show?

5. Which British queen's picture appeared on the first postage stamps?

6. Who is the Celtic earth goddess?

7. What was the name given to the group of women who worked together to further the cause of women and their rights in the early part of the last century?

8. In which country is the soap opera 'Neighbours' set?

Answers on page 109

ROUND 7

1. Name the astronaut who at the age of 77 travelled to space for the second time?

2. According to the proverb, what is the mother of invention?

3. Who wrote the books *The Van* and *The Commitments*?

4. If you were coming in for a 'Pit Stop', what sport would you be participating in?

5. In which county are the towns of Maynooth and Celbridge?

6. What is the capital of Venezuela?

7. The sons of Míl were known as Milesians or by what other name?

8. How often are brain cells replaced?

Answers on page 110

ROUND 8

1. What is the Red Cross called in Arab Countries?

2. What actor links the films *Thelma and Louise*, *The Curious Case of Benjamin Button* and *Moneyball*?

3. When Ireland became a member of the European Community on 1 January 1973, what other two countries joined on the same day?

4. By what name is Richard de Clare, Earl of Pembroke, better known in Irish history?

5. What scale measures the force of wind?

6. What is the English meaning of *Táin Bó Cúailnge*?

7. How many feet in a fathom?

8. What is the main ingredient of Coke?

Answers on page 110

ROUND 9

1. What is the last letter of the Greek alphabet?

2. What river passes more water back into the sea than any other?

3. How many bones does an adult have?

4. The Maple Leaf is the national symbol of which country?

5. Who created Winnie the Pooh?

6. What do the letters D.A.R.T. stand for (as in the Dublin train network)?

7. In what English city were all the members of the Beatles pop group born?

8. Name the only man-made object which can be seen from space?

Answers on page 110

Round 10

1. What are the two main colours of the flag of Spain?

2. What game does William Porterfield play?

3. Which country was ruled by Peter the Great and Catherine the Great?

4. In the Bible, name the criminal whom the crowd asked to be released instead of Jesus?

5. What do the emu, ostrich and kiwi have in common?

6. What South African was released from prison after 28 years in February 1990?

7. What is the meat of a deer called?

8. How many points are awarded for scoring a try in rugby union?

Answers on page 110

Quiz Number 7

Round 1

1. The sun is a star. True or false?

2. Name the three girls in the TV series 'Friends'.

3. From which crop do we get flour?

4. In a deck of cards, which way does the Jack of Hearts usually face?

5. If it is 23 hours in Ireland, what time is it in New York? Is it 6pm, 7pm or 8pm?

6. Alexander Fleming invented what drug?

7. In which continent did the Cree tribe live?

8. What name is given to the process by which a liquid is turned into gas?

Answers on page 110

ROUND 2

1. Name the three farmers in Roald Dahl's *Fantastic Mr Fox*?

2. Who was the first person to reach the North Pole?

3. In which country did Sumo wrestling originate?

4. What colour are the corner squares of a scrabble board?

5. On which river is the city of Kilkenny built?

6. For the discovery of what were Marie and Pierre Curie awarded the Nobel prize for in 1903?

7. What name is given to New York's financial district?

8. What do the words *haute couture* mean?

Answers on page 110

ROUND 3

1. Can you finish the title of the play by Shakespeare, *The Merchant of*...?

2. In the Harry Potter series, what kind of animal is Buckbeak?

3. What common wild animal looks like a long-legged rabbit?

4. Which is the larger town in County Louth – Dundalk or Drogheda?

5. What famous Hollywood star survived a plane crash in 2015?

6. Which weighs the most, a cubic metre of ice or a cubic metre of water?

7. What job does an apiarist do?

8. Isabella of Castille and Ferdinand of Aragon united which European country on their marriage?

Answers on page 110

ROUND 4

1. How many men did the Grand Old Duke of York march up and down the hill?

2. What name is given to a tiny gelatine shell containing medicine?

3. What precious gem can be found in some oysters?

4. In Greek mythology, name the creature which was half horse, half man?

5. Which period in Irish history was known as the Emergency?

6. What do fish breathe through?

7. How many points should the winner have at the end of a set in table tennis?

8. In what year was the *Titanic* built in Belfast – (a) 1906; (b) 1908; (c) 1912?

Answers on page 111

Round 5

1. Milady de Winter was the deadly enemy of which fictional heroes?

2. If you add XL and LX in roman numerals what is the answer, also in roman numerals?

3. Who was the only Irish President to die in office?

4. In air traffic and police communication, the letter A is followed by the word ALPHA. What word follows the letter D?

5. In Irish mythology, who ordered the raid on the Brown Bull of Cooley?

6. What actor was the voice of Buzz Lightyear?

7. What is a male rabbit called?

8. Must polo players be right-handed, left-handed or able to use both hands?

Answers on page 111

ROUND 6

1. How many lines has a Limerick?

2. Which famous detective lived in the village of St Mary Mead?

3. Who executed the double agent, Mata Hari, during the First World War, the French or the Germans?

4. What is a bog pimpernel – (a) a bird; (b) a wild fox; (c) a flower?

5. Which Greek god was famous for his pipe music?

6. Which of the following states is the biggest – San Marino, Monaco, or the Vatican?

7. What is the capital of Cameroon?

8. What happens to water when it reaches 100 degrees celsius?

Answers on page 111

ROUND 7

1. Riga is the capital of which of the Baltic states, Latvia, Lithuania or Estonia?

2. Which planet is furthest away from the sun?

3. What was Timmy of the Famous Five?

4. Which chess piece can you move as many squares as you like, in any direction?

5. Is the goalkeeper allowed to score in a soccer match?

6. Which country produces the most bananas?

7. Name the sea that divides northeast Ireland from Scotland – (a) St George's Channel (b) North Channel (c) Atlantic Ocean?

8. How many batsmen play at the same time in a cricket match?

Answers on page 111

Round 8

1. What is the female equivalent of a Sultan?

2. In Gaelic football and hurling, how many points is a goal worth?

3. Which very famous duck was 80 years old in 2014?

4. Arderin is the highest peak in what mountain range?

5. What is the collective term for a group of owls – (a) murder; (b) pride or (c) parliament?

6. What is the capital of Mongolia?

7. How many runs are there in a cricket century?

8. Who is the Roman god of water and the sea?

Answers on page 111

Round 9

1. Which of the apostles was the brother of St Peter?

2. Name the leader of the 1803 rebellion who was arrested and hanged despite the refusal of his associate Anne Devlin to give evidence against him?

3. What nationality was the composer Bizet?

4. What countries make up the Iberian Peninsula?

5. What is the largest town in County Tipperary?

6. Name three original members of the band One Direction.

7. This Greek goddess of victory shares her name with a famous brand of sports gear/sportswear?

8. On the side of what lake does Killarney stand?

Answers on page 111

Round 10

1. Which is the smallest (1) the earth, (b) the sun or (c) the moon?

2. Who designed the process of killing disease-producing micro-organisms in food and drink?

3. Where are the Partry Mountains?

4. What do the letters CND stand for?

5. The Merry Widow is a type of spider. True or false?

6. Carrots are root vegetables, cabbage is a leafy vegetable. What very common vegetable is known as a tuber?

7. Which chess piece can jump over others?

8. In what year did Pope John Paul II visit Ireland – 1969, 1970 or 1979?

Answers on page 112

QUIZ NUMBER 8

ROUND 1

1. What do the letters UNICEF stand for?

2. What is the capital of Portugal?

3. Who was the fat, jovial monk of Robin Hood's Band of Merry Men?

4. Name the world's bestselling book?

5. In which county are the Blue Stack Mountains?

6. What sporting event commemorates Cuchulainn's journey through the Cooley Mountains on his way to Ulster?

7. What name is given to the mixture of gases we breath?

8. Larry Mullen and Adam Clayton are members of which Irish group?

Answers on page 112

ROUND 2

1. At what age does lamb become mutton?

2. What colours are on Monaco's flag?

3. What Government department is in charge of Met Éireann??

4. What colour jersey does the leader of the Tour de France wear?

5. What is the main symptom of asthma?

6. What star sign is represented by a weighing scales?

7. In what year did Mary Robinson become president of Ireland?

8. What is the black lace veil traditionally worn by Spanish ladies called?

Answers on page 112

ROUND 3

1. In judo, what is the colour of a beginners belt?

2. Who was the first person to develop practical radio equipment?

3. Where did St Patrick land in Ireland – (a) Carrickfergus, County Antrim; (b) Saul, County Down or (c) Drogheda, County Louth?

4. Which is the body's largest glandular organ?

5. In Greek mythology, where was the house of the gods?

6. Where would you find Christmas Island?

7. What do you call the craft in which astronauts return to earth from space?

8. What was the name given to the group of people who raided and destroyed monasteries and settlements in Ireland during the ninth and tenth centuries?

Answers on page 112

ROUND 4

1. Who plays Mr Bean in the television series and film of the same name?

2. What famous Irishman was known as King of the Beggars?

3. Which country has the largest land mass in the world?

4. What is a male swan called?

5. What is the name given to gases that float up into the clouds, join with water droplets in the clouds and fall to earth?

6. Before they became the Beatles, what were they called?

7. What is the usual colour for the centre of a dartboard?

8. In which African country is Casablanca?

Answers on page 113

ROUND 5

1. What name is given to a bicycle made for two people?

2. Do bananas grow in clusters called hands, knees or feet?

3. What are canines and incisors?

4. Black, yellow and red are the colours of the German Flag. What other western European Country has the same colours on its flag?

5. Whose voice was used for the donkey in 'Shrek'?

6. What do you call a song in praise of God?

7. What is the name of the official anthem of the United States of America?

8. Who was the first sportsman to be given the freedom of Dublin – (a) Sean Kelly; (b) Stephen Roche; (c) Jack Charlton?

Answers on page 113

Round 6

1. What do you make models from if your hobby is origami?

2. On what lake did the children of Lir spend 300 years?

3. Name the bird that sprang from its own ashes.

4. Tripoli is the capital of which North African country?

5. If you were born on 9 May, what would your star sign be?

6. What kind of hats did Laurel and Hardy wear?

7. Blood returns to your heart through your veins. Through what channels is blood pumped AWAY from the heart?

8. In ancient Ireland, what was a skib – (a) a woven basket; (b) a sword or (c) a type of boat?

Answers on page 113

ROUND 7

1. How many pieces of leather make the outside of a cricket ball?

2. For what invention is Rudolf Diesel best known?

3. Who, according to the Bible, lived to be 969 years old and thus became the oldest man of all times?

4. Who wrote the novel *Wuthering Heights*?

5. Where in Ireland were *crannógs* built?

6. Is a fully-grown giraffe 3-4 metres, 5-6 metres or 7-8 metres in height?

7. The country of Monaco is surrounded by which EU country?

8. Name the only racecourse in County Kilkenny?

Answers on page 113

ROUND 8

1. In which century were Louis XVI and Marie Antoinette guillotined?

2. What symbol is used by all Government Departments in Ireland?

3. On what date does Women's Christmas fall?

4. What is the second book of the Bible?

5. The orang-utan is found on which continent?

6. What does a phanophobic fear?

7. Bunratty Castle is in what county?

8. Which mammal can fly?

Answers on page 113

Round 9

1. What is the highest mountain peak in the Alps?

2. What city inspired the song 'The Town I loved so well'?

3. What is the smallest Irish mammal?

4. Name the species of birds, now extinct, which lived on the island of Mauritius for tens of thousands of years?

5. How many O.W.L.s did Hermione receive?

6. What river flows through the city of Liverpool in England?

7. Why were Wilbur and Orville Wright famous?

8. Into what sea does the River Danube flow?

Answers on page 113

Round 10

1. What British Admiral was killed at the Battle of Trafalgar?

2. In Greek mythology, name the female monster with a human head and the body of a lion?

3. What is the largest planet in the solar system?

4. How many stripes are there on Adidas sports clothing?

5. Who was known as 'The Big Fellow' in Irish politics?

6. What is the meaning of the word bibliophile?

7. 'The pale moon was rising ...' is the first line of a song associated with what Irish festival?

8. In which European city would you find the Trevi Fountain?

Answers on page 113

Quiz Number 9

Round 1

1. Name the Simpson cartoon family.

2. In what county is Crag Cave?

3. Who is the patron saint of Scotland?

4. Do stalagmites come from the roof or the floor of a cave?

5. What colour is a female blackbird?

6. In which county do the Mountains of Mourne sweep down to the sea?

7. What is the capital of Poland?

8. Which tropic is north of the Equator – is it the Tropic of Capricorn or the Tropic of Cancer?

Answers on page 114

Round 2

1. Where are the Nephin Beg Mountains?

2. What hand do scouts shake hands with?

3. Which superhero was born on the planet Krypton?

4. How many countries border Germany?

5. With what historical movement are John Calvin, Martin Luther and King Henry Vlll associated?

6. In ancient Ireland, what was a gallowglass?

7. Name the wild Australian dog?

8. What country's flag features a light blue star of David?

Answers on page 114

ROUND 3

1. In the Disney film, what breed of dogs did Cruella de Ville kidnap?

2. What is the subject matter of the Book of Kells?

3. Which famous waterfall is on the border between the USA and Canada?

4. What kind of animal is a flying fox?

5. Who wrote *A Tale of Two Cities*?

6. What river flows through Galway?

7. From what plant do we get linen?

8. What name is given to the Earth's satellite?

Answers on page 114

Round 4

1. What animal's name means 'riverhorse'?

2. What flower means 'The first rose of spring'?

3. How many rings are there on the Olympic Symbol?

4. Name the lost continent, a paradise on earth, that according to legend is under the Atlantic?

5. What name is given to joining metal objects by melting their edges so that they fuse together?

6. In what year was the Boston Tea Party?

7. The remains of what sea animal are common in bathrooms?

8. How many queen bees live in a hive?

Answers on page 114

Round 5

1. What letter of the alphabet is marked on a snooker table?

2. In what county are the towns of Drogheda, Dundalk and Ardee?

3. What sauce is traditionally served with roast pork?

4. What is the capital city of India?

5. What is calligraphy?

6. What is unusual about a manx cat?

7. What is the name given to the day before Ash Wednesday?

8. Near what Australian city is the famous Bondi Beach?

Answers on page 114

ROUND 6

1. How many children had Lír?

2. Name the children of Lír?

3. On a guitar, is the lowest note played by the thinnest or the thickest string?

4. What word describes tiny droplets of water suspended in the air close to the ground surface?

5. What kind of birds are the biggest in the world?

6. Who put Humpty Dumpty together again?

7. What do rugby players and boxers often have in their mouths that is made of plastic?

8. How many miles long is Ireland's coastline?

Answers on page 114

Round 7

1. What kind of light operates a solar panel?

2. Which is the biggest county in Northern Ireland?

3. Which baby in the Bible was found in the bull rushes?

4. In politics, what do the letters MEP stand for?

5. What singer had a hit with 'If I Were a Boy'?

6. The bright face of the Moon turns dark when it passes into the Earth's shadow. What word describes this phenomenon?

7. What did Jason have to do to win back his father's kingdom of Iolcos?

8. Name the author of the book *Under the Hawthorn Tree*.

Answers on page 115

ROUND 8

1. In which sport does the winning team move backwards?

2. Who was the first man to reach the South Pole?

3. Name the Irish family group who had hit singles with songs like 'Runaway' and 'Forgiven not Forgotten'?

4. The month of July is named after which Roman Emperor?

5. Where is Queen's University?

6. If your birthday fell on 1 September, what would your star sign be?

7. Who wrote the novel *Strumpet City*?

8. Are skis chalked, scratched or waxed?

Answers on page 115

ROUND 9

1. What is the capital city of Argentina?

2. In what county was St Brigid born?

3. What liquid is given an octane number?

4. Which part of your body is most likely to suffer from chilblains?

5. Which would be the hottest, a star, a planet or a comet?

6. What famous castle did Lord Gort present to the Irish people?

7. Which French president has an airport named after him?

8. In the book of Genesis, on which day did God create light?

Answers on page 115

Round 10

1. If you committed patricide, what would you have done?

2. What creature's home is called a drey?

3. In which country would you find the original Legoland?

4. Which is heavier, a kilo of feathers or a kilo of chocolate?

5. By what name was Cassius Clay better known?

6. What do the letters ERM stand for?

7. Name the Indian river which is sacred to the followers of the Hindu religion?

8. What kind of sportsperson would practice by jumping a cavaletti?

Answers on page 115

QUIZ NUMBER 10

ROUND 1

1. World Champion athlete Sonia O'Sullivan is a native of which County Cork town?

2. What did the Little Mermaid exchange her voice for?

3. Name the vehicle registration code for Kilkenny?

4. In what county is the town of Caherciveen?

5. How many earthquakes occur every day – (a) more than 20; (b) more than 200 or (c) more than 1,000

6. Professor Plum, Miss Scarlet, Miss White and Colonel Mustard are all characters from which board game?

7. Does an insomniac have difficulty sleeping, hearing or remembering?

8. Who wrote the novels *The Man in the Iron Mask* and *The Three Musketeers*?

Answers on page 116

ROUND 2

1. What is the top division in the English football league called?

2. Is there such a thing as Acid Snow?

3. What is the capital of Iraq?

4. In which century did Columbus first reach America?

5. What is the second smallest county in Ireland?

6. What is the staple food for more than half the world?

7. How many squares are there on a draughts board?

8. What are the four main points of the compass?

Answers on page 116

Round 3

1. What animal punch would you associate with karate?

2. What Battle between the Greeks and the Persians in ancient times gives its name to an athletic event?

3. What series of films and TV programmes feature Mr Spock?

4. Is there a soccer team called Sheffield Tuesday, Sheffield Wednesday or Sheffield Thursday?

5. What year was the Marriage Equality Act passed?

6. What is the capital of Surinam?

7. What is the largest reptile?

8. Haggis is a famous food in which country?

Answers on page 116

ROUND 4

1. How many pockets has a billiard table?

2. To what were sailors referring to when they spoke of Davy Jones Locker?

3. New York City is the capital of New York State. True or false?

4. According to the nursery rhyme, what frightened Miss Muffat?

5. In what county does the Shannon rise?

6. Name Oisín's son?

7. Who was Popeye's girlfriend?

8. The largest mammal in the world is the elephant. True or false?

Answers on page 116

ROUND 5

1. Wine is made from the juice of what fruit?

2. How many years is the normal term of office of the president of Ireland?

3. Who was the mother of John the Baptist?

4. What are Gilbert and Sullivan famous for?

5. What Dublin street was once called Sackville Street?

6. From what animal is veal obtained?

7. What sport uses epées to duel?

8. Who wrote *The Ugly Duckling* and *The Little Mermaid*?

Answers on page 116

ROUND 6

1. On what mountain did Moses receive the Ten Commandments?

2. What is the name of London's largest airport?

3. Name the Greek giant who had one eye and a taste for human flesh?

4. Which English ruler ordered the execution of Mary Queen of Scots, who was accused of plotting to take over the throne of England?

5. What are the first names of the Patil twins in the Harry Potter series?

6. In which county are the towns of Bundoran and Killybegs?

7. On what river is Paris built?

8. Which fish is spawned in the Sargasso Sea?

Answers on page 116

ROUND 7

1. How many squares are there on one side of a Rubik's cube?

2. Who was known as the Hound of Ulster?

3. What is the Brownie motto?

4. How many points are scored between each change of service in table tennis?

5. Saab cars originate in what country?

6. Which Austrian composer is best known for his work, 'The Blue Danube'?

7. In the Bible what was the occupation of the apostles James and John?

8. In computer terms, what do the letters ROM mean?

Answers on page 117

Round 8

1. How many cards are there in a pack, not including the Jokers?

2. Meg, Jo, Amy and Beth are the main characters in which book written by Louisa M. Alcott?

3. What do you call a male bee?

4. What percentage of the earth's water is drinkable?

5. Name the author of *The Iron Man and the Iron Woman*?

6. Which crabs have no shell of their own?

7. These are often called the food factories of green plants. What is their most common name?

8. Name Fionn MacCumhaill's army?

Answers on page 117

ROUND 9

1. What name is given to 1 November?

2. Which Irish county is known as the Banner County?

3. Who was known as the 'lady of the lamp'?

4. What bone is made up of several vertebrae?

5. What suburb of Galway is a popular tourist destination?

6. What is the singular of Scampi?

7. In what decade was the Barbie doll first produced – the 1950s, 1960s or 1980s?

8. Name the famous Celtic brooch on display at the National Museum?

Answers on page 117

Round 10

1. On which river are Victoria Falls?

2. What was the sequel to *Little Women*?

3. Who defeated Napoleon at Waterloo?

4. What is the popular name for the crane fly?

5. Name the Irishman who won the Tour de France?

6. Which is further south, Moscow or Stockholm?

7. There are 100,000,000,000 stars in our galaxy. What name is given to our galaxy?

8. Name the Irish painter whose brother was a famous poet?

Answers on page 117

QUIZ ANSWERS

QUIZ NUMBER 1

ROUND 1
1. Genoa
2. 18.45
3. A pirate ship
4. Setanta
5. A bear
6. Mount Errigal
7. Fitzgerald
8. Record, disc.

ROUND 2
1. Canary
2. Bruce Wayne
3. DNA
4. Theseus
5. 1845
6. The Battle of Kinsale
7. Aries
8. Diagonally

ROUND 3
1. 2016
2. Fionn MacCumhaill
3. *The Force Awakens'*
4. Donegal
5. Comes out at night/hunts at night/active by night
6. Second World War
7. Saves nine
8. Pyramids

ROUND 4
1. Primary School Teachers
2. Galway
3. Herbivores
4. W.B. Yeats
5. Oslo
6. Ran away with the spoon
7. The ear
8. M

ROUND 5
1. Lowest Common Multiple
2. A winged horse
3. Antrim
4. Insulin
5. The White House
6. Seven
7. O'Neill
8. A humming bird

ROUND 6
1. Yuri Gagarin
2. *A Christmas Carol*
3. Seven
4. Electronic
5. James Bond
6. The Mona Lisa
7. Galway
8. New York

Round 7
1. William Wordsworth
2. £200
3. Capricorn
4. Niamh
5. Sir Humphrey Davy
6. *The Way That I Love You*
7. Golf
8. Mrs Trunchbull

Round 8
1. Robbie Brady
2. German
3. The Dead Sea
4. Temperature
5. Sir Walter Raleigh
6. A pumpkin
7. St David
8. Finneagas

Round 9
1. Africa
2. Wexford
3. Heronries
4. 061
5. Pigments
6. Lamb
7. Pontypandy
8. Slane (County Meath)

Round 10
1. The Flight of the Earls
2. Enid Blyton
3. Six
4. Eighteen
5. Bandon
6. The Boyne
7. Kanye West and Kim Kardashian
8. Martin O'Neill

ROUND 1
1. The wren
2. The middle
3. Charles Darwin
4. 47
5. 'Home and Away'
6. The Tropic of Capricorn
7. Central Europe
8. Donegal

ROUND 2
1. Lara Croft
2. Linseed
3. County Cork
4. Potholing/speleology
5. Great Britain in 1840
6. William Wallace
7. Quadruped
8. Nairobi

ROUND 3
1. A stone
2. County Wicklow
3. The lungs
4. A colt
5. Eight
6. A grape
7. 1947
8. In his hair

ROUND 4
1. Twenty
2. Antananarivo
3. The Hague
4. Oysters
5. The Donkey
6. The bodhrán or drums
7. C.S. Lewis
8. Egypt

ROUND 5
1. Jerusalem
2. Tipperary
3. Nottingham Forest
4. *Go raibh maith agat*
5. Abraham Lincoln
6. National Parents Council-Primary
7. Celeste
8. 100

ROUND 6
1. Average
2. Greenland
3. Simba
4. A billy goat
5. Fermanagh
6. Jim Davis
7. The Gestapo
8. Thursday

ROUND 7
1. Five
2. Hobart
3. Earthworms
4. 32
5. Basketball
6. A crotchet
7. County Mayo
8. Geysers

ROUND 8
1. Charles Stewart Parnell
2. Blue and yellow
3. The unicorn
4. J.R.R. Tolkien
5. On a gravestone
6. Robert Emmet
7. No
8. Acupuncture

ROUND 9
1. Edelweiss
2. Pawns
3. River Suir
4. Quinton Blake
5. Margaret Thatcher
6. Gold
7. Westmeath
8. Venus

ROUND 10
1. Robin Hood
2. Roald Dahl
3. John Logie Baird
4. Dave Evans
5. Leinster (Dublin)
6. Pontius Pilate
7. Cearbhall O'Dálaigh
8. Jack Lynch Tunnel

QUIZ NUMBER 3

ROUND 1
1. A calf
2. A banana
3. England
4. September
5. Steven Spielberg
6. A hovercraft
7. Japan
8. Shaggy, Fred, Velma and Daphne

ROUND 2
1. Christopher Columbus
2. Highest Common Factor
3. 'is the hand that rules the world'
4. A spider
5. Penguins
6. England
7. Lábhraigh Loingseach
8. Because he had horse's ears

ROUND 3
1. Spring and autumn
2. Journey/tour
3. Sherlock Holmes
4. a = 36
5. Rob Heffernan
6. Braille
7. Canberra
8. Wicklow

ROUND 4
1. The Rovers Return
2. The Arctic; the Indian; the Southern/Antarctic Ocean
3. A fruit
4. Dr Douglas Hyde
5. Arizona
6. By flying – he fixed wings to his arms with wax
7. House of Lords
8. Bastille Day

ROUND 5
1. A tadpole
2. The Queen of Sheba
3. The flute
4. Prague
5. Neck
6. Limerick
7. President John F. Kennedy
8. Horticulture

ROUND 6
1. Glen Hansard
2. North
3. The Lions
4. *Treasure Island*
5. African
6. Galway
7. South America
8. Cecelia Ahern

ROUND 7
1. Harry Potter
2. Eighth
3. Romulus and Remus
4. *The Titanic*
5. Loss of smell
6. 8,100
7. County Kerry
8. 1981

ROUND 8
1. A bridge
2. Matthew's Gospel
3. Mizen Head
4. Eamon de Valera
5. Mercury
6. 1961
7. Africa
8. Dans

ROUND 9
1. Four years
2. On the moon
3. Kildare
4. Mary Shelley
5. Greece
6. Guinevere
7. Lahinch
8. Angelina Jolie

ROUND 10
1. *The Bounty*
2. Secretary General
3. Bulgaria
4. Twelve
5. Perfume
6. The Severn
7. Neil Armstrong
8. Mars

Quiz Number 4

Round 1
1. Tír na nÓg
2. Lewis Carroll
3. A kiwi
4. Waterford
5. An elver
6. Vitamin D
7. Football
8. Fionn MacCumhaill

Round 2
1. Red, orange, yellow, green, blue, indigo, violet
2. A mammal
3. Computer
4. Lough Neagh
5. France
6. Kerry
7. Sound
8. Divination

Round 3
1. The Ice Age
2. Carbon dioxide
3. Pisa
4. Bedrock
5. A puck goat
6. Advent
7. Ann Martin
8. Armagh

Round 4
1. Athens
2. 'its weakest link'
3. Lettuce
4. Tennis
5. Pluto
6. A cow
7. Van Houten
8. Rathlin Island

Round 5
1. 'Neighbours'
2. *Scamaill*
3. Loss of memory
4. Suzanne Collins
5. 1291
6. Majorca
7. Jamie Suzan
8. First World War (1914-1918)

Round 6
1. Scotland
2. Napoleon Bonaparte
3. Brian Friel
4. Southeast
5. 1014
6. Eros
7. x = 15
8. The study of fossils

Round 7
1. George W. Bush
2. Jasper or Horace
3. County Cork
4. Mercury
5. Homer (a Greek poet)
6. Cheese
7. Dun Laoghaire
8. Golf

ROUND 8
1. The thistle
2. Agatha Christie
3. 1979
4. A light year
5. Quito
6. Three
7. Runs
8. Anna Sewell

ROUND 9
1. A school
2. Down
3. The heart
4. The Chancellor of the Exchequer
5. Florida
6. Seamus Heaney
7. Clonmacnoise
8. Norway

ROUND 10
1. St Bernadette
2. Hieroglyphics
3. L
4. It uses the shadows cast by the sun
5. The wings
6. A fossil
7. Aslan
8. India

QUIZ NUMBER 5

ROUND 1
1. The Simpsons
2. Vixen
3. Tipperary
4. New York
5. *Oliver!*
6. Cuchulainn
7. Amelia Earhart
8. One

ROUND 2
1. Soot
2. They are all whales
3. Latitude
4. Dick Whittington
5. Vienna
6. Jane Austen
7. Bashful
8. The black

ROUND 3
1. Eight
2. The sloe
3. *David Copperfield*
4. Horology
5. A magic spear used by
   Cuchulainn to kill Ferdia
6. Nine
7. The Panama Canal
8. Veronica

ROUND 4
1. (a) a shoe
2. Monday
3. Austria
4. An ostrich
5. South Africa
6. The hip or the shoulder
7. A holt
8. Turned to stone

ROUND 5
1. Achill Island
2. (b) in your leg (kneecap)
3. Beef or lamb
4. Wellington
5. Robert Emmet
6. Julian, George, Dick, Ann,
   Timmy the dog
7. 'Fair City'
8. Massachusetts, USA

ROUND 6
1. A priest
2. 24
3. 25 years
4. N11
5. Zeus
6. The Philippines
7. Bitzer
8. Walk in your sleep (sleepwalker)

ROUND 7
1. Butter
2. Aquarius
3. Miley Cyrus
4. Alfred Nobel
5. Ennis
6. 25
7. Old Testament
8. County Mayo

ROUND 8
1. Chloraflurocarbons
2. Russia
3. Brussels
4. Cattle
5. Buzz Aldrin
6. Brian O'Driscoll
7. Absent Without Official Leave
8. Piano

ROUND 9
1. Antarctica
2. The pupil
3. Six
4. Lugnacaille (Lugnaguilla)
5. Migration
6. A leaf
7. King Solomon
8. Alaska

ROUND 10
1. Eight
2. Blue
3. St Brendan
4. Brains
5. The trumpet
6. Italian cheese
7. At the wedding in Cana
8. Sue Townsend

Quiz Number 6

Round 1
1. Take That
2. Aldi
3. *An bhó/bó*
4. Stephanie Meyer
5. Rome
6. The Gaelic League/Connradh na Gaeilge
7. 1789
8. Aintree

Round 2
1. Juventus
2. Samuel Morse
3. Spraints
4. Joey
5. A hen
6. Sofia
7. A modem
8. True

Round 3
1. Daniel Craig
2. Camelot
3. Italy
4. Phases
5. Paris
6. Welcome
7. Mullingar
8. Denmark

Round 4
1. *The Golden Hind*
2. Cleopatra
3. 1920s
4. The earth
5. Poland
6. Butterflies
7. City
8. Credit cards

Round 5
1. Will Turner
2. Tentacles
3. Golf
4. Kitty
5. Grace Kelly
6. Innisheer
7. 1690
8. A vacuum

Round 6
1. R.L. Stine
2. The pyramids of Egypt
3. River Lagan
4. 'The Muppet Show'
5. Queen Victoria
6. Danu
7. Suffragettes
8. Australia

ROUND 7
1. John Glenn
2. Necessity
3. Roddy Doyle
4. Motor Racing
5. Kildare
6. Caracas
7. The Gaels
8. Never

ROUND 8
1. The Red Crescent
2. Brad Pitt
3. UK and Denmark
4. Strongbow
5. The Beaufort wind scale
6. The Cattle Raid of Cooley
7. Six feet
8. Sugar

ROUND 9
1. Omega
2. The Amazon
3. 206
4. Canada
5. A.A. Milne
6. Dublin Area Rapid Transit
7. Liverpool
8. The Great Wall of China

ROUND 10
1. Yellow and red
2. Cricket
3. Russia
4. Barabbas
5. They cannot fly
6. Nelson Mandela
7. Venison
8. Five

QUIZ NUMBER 7

ROUND 1
1. True
2. Monica, Rachel and Phoebe
3. Wheat
4. Right
5. 6pm
6. Penicillin
7. America
8. Evaporation

ROUND 2
1. Boggis, Bunce, Bean
2. Robert Peary
3. Japan
4. Red
5. The Nore
6. Radium
7. Wall Street
8. High fashion

ROUND 3
1. Venice
2. A hippogriff
3. The hare
4. Dundalk
5. Harrison Ford
6. A cubic metre of water
7. Keeps bees
8. Spain

ROUND 4
1. 10,000
2. A capsule
3. Pearl
4. Centaur
5. The Second World War
6. Gills
7. 21
8. 1912

ROUND 5
1. The Three Musketeers
2. C
3. Erskine Childers
4. Delta
5. Queen Maebh of Connacht
6. Tim Allen
7. Buck
8. Right-handed

ROUND 6
1. Five
2. Miss Marple
3. The French
4. A flower
5. Pan
6. San Marino
7. Yaoundé
8. It starts to boil

ROUND 7
1. Latvia
2. Pluto
3. A dog
4. The queen
5. Yes
6. Brazil
7. The North Channel
8. Two

ROUND 8
1. A Sultana
2. Three
3. Donald Duck
4. Slieve Bloom Mountains
5. Parliament
6. Ulan Bator
7. 100
8. Neptune

ROUND 9
1. St Andrew
2. Robert Emmet
3. French
4. Spain and Portugal
5. Clonmel
6. Niall Horan, Liam Payne, Harry Styles, Louis Tomlinson, Zayn Malik
7. Nike
8. Lough Leane

ROUND 10
1. Moon
2. Louis Pasteur
3. Mayo
4. Campaign for Nuclear Disarmament
5. False (black widow is the spider; *The Merry Widow* is an operetta)
6. The potato
7. Knight
8. 1979

QUIZ NUMBER 8

ROUND 1
1. United Nations International Children's Emergency Fund
2. Lisbon
3. Friar Tuck
4. The Bible
5. County Donegal
6. Poc Fada Competition
7. Air
8. U2

ROUND 2
1. One
2. Red and white
3. Department of the Environment, Community and Local Government
4. Yellow
5. Wheezing
6. Libra
7. 1990
8. Mantilla

ROUND 3
1. White
2. Marconi
3. (b) Saul, County Down
4. The liver
5. Olympus
6. Indian Ocean
7. A shuttle
8. The Vikings

ROUND 4
1. Rowan Atkinson
2. Daniel O'Connell
3. Russia
4. A cob
5. Acid rain
6. The Quarrymen
7. Red
8. Morocco

ROUND 5
1. A tandem
2. Hands
3. Teeth
4. Belgium
5. Eddie Murphy
6. A hymn
7. The Star Spangled Banner
8. Stephen Roche

ROUND 6
1. Paper
2. Lake Darravaragh
3. The phoenix
4. Libya
5. Taurus
6. Bowler Hats
7. Arteries
8. (a) a woven basket

ROUND 7
1. Two
2. The diesel engine
3. Methusaleh
4. Emily Brontë
5. In the middle of lakes
6. 5-6 metres
7. France
8. Gowran Park

ROUND 8
1. Eighteen
2. The harp
3. 6 January
4. Exodus
5. Asia
6. Noise
7. Clare
8. The bat

ROUND 9
1. Mont Blanc
2. Derry
3. Pygmy shrew
4. The dodo
5. Eleven (ten Outstanding and one Exceeds Expectations)
6. The Mersey
7. They made the first flight in a powered airplane in 1903
8. The Black Sea

ROUND 10
1. Nelson
2. Sphinx
3. Jupiter
4. Three
5. Michael Collins
6. A person who collects or is fond of books
7. The Rose of Tralee
8. Rome

Quiz Number 9

Round 1
1. Homer, Marge, Bart, Lisa and Maggie
2. County Kerry
3. St Andrew
4. The floor
5. Brown
6. County Down
7. Warsaw
8. The Tropic of Cancer

Round 2
1. Mayo
2. The left
3. Superman
4. Nine
5. The Reformation
6. A soldier
7. The dingo
8. Israel

Round 3
1. Dalmations
2. The four Gospels
3. Niagara Falls
4. A species of bat
5. Charles Dickens
6. The Corrib
7. Flax
8. The Moon

Round 4
1. Hippopotamus
2. The primrose
3. Five
4. Atlantis
5. Welding
6. 1773
7. A sponge
8. One

Round 5
1. D
2. County Louth
3. Apple sauce
4. Delhi
5. The craft of handwriting
6. It has no tail
7. Shrove Tuesday
8. Sydney

Round 6
1. Four
2. Fionnuala, Aodh, Fiachra and Conn
3. The thickest string
4. Fog
5. Ostriches
6. Nobody
7. Gum shields
8. 3,500 miles

ROUND 7
1. Sunlight
2. Tyrone
3. Moses
4. Member of the European Parliament
5. Beyoncé
6. Eclipse or lunar eclipse
7. Steal the golden fleece which the dragon guarded
8. Marita Conlon-McKenna

ROUND 8
1. Tug o' war
2. Roald Amundsen in 1911
3. The Corrs
4. Julius Caesar
5. Belfast
6. Virgo
7. James Plunkett
8. Waxed

ROUND 9
1. Buenos Aires
2. County Louth
3. Petrol
4. Your fingers and toes
5. A star
6. Bunratty
7. Charles de Gaulle
8. On the first day

ROUND 10
1. Killed your father
2. A squirrel
3. Denmark
4. They both weigh the same
5. Muhammad Ali
6. Exchange Rate Mechanism
7. Ganges
8. A horse or pony rider

ROUND 1
1. Cobh
2. Legs
3. KK
4. Kerry
5. (c) more than 1,000
6. Cluedo
7. Sleeping
8. Alexandre Dumas

ROUND 2
1. The Premiership
2. Yes
3. Baghdad
4. Fifteenth
5. Carlow
6. Rice
7. 64
8. North, south, east and west

ROUND 3
1. Rabbit
2. The Battle of Marathon, 1490 BC
3. Star Trek
4. Sheffield Wednesday
5. 2015
6. Paramaribo
7. Crocodile
8. Scotland

ROUND 4
1. Six
2. The bottom of the sea
3. False (Albany is the capital)
4. A spider
5. County Cavan
6. Oscar
7. Olive Oyl
8. False (the blue whale is the largest mammal)

ROUND 5
1. The grape
2. Seven years
3. Elizabeth
4. They wrote light comic operas
5. O'Connell Street
6. Calf
7. Fencing
8. Hans Christian Anderson

ROUND 6
1. Mount Sinai
2. Heathrow
3. Cyclops
4. Elizabeth I
5. Padma and Parvati
6. Donegal
7. The Seine
8. Eel

ROUND 7
1. Nine
2. Cuchulainn
3. 'Lend a Hand'
4. Five
5. Sweden
6. Johann Strauss
7. Fishermen
8. Read Only Memory

ROUND 8
1. 52
2. *Little Women*
3. A drone
4. One per cent
5. Ted Hughes
6. Hermit Crab
7. Leaves
8. Na Fianna

ROUND 9
1. All Saints' Day
2. Clare
3. Florence Nightingale
4. The backbone
5. Salthill
6. Scamp
7. 1950s (1959)
8. The Tara brooch

ROUND 10
1. Zambezi
2. *Good Wives*
3. The Duke of Wellington
4. Daddy Long Legs
5. Stephen Roche
6. Moscow
7. The Milky Way
8. Jack B. Yeats

If you have enjoyed *The Whiz Quiz Book*,
why not try *More Whiz Quiz*?

Available at all good bookshops and online at
www.collinspress.ie

MORE WHIZ QUIZ

For Children and Grown-up Children

MORE WHIZ QUIZ

The Collins Press